JUAN SEGUÍN
TEJANO LEADER

WILLIAM R. CHEMERKA
ILLUSTRATIONS BY
DON COLLINS

bright sky press
HOUSTON, TEXAS

bright sky press
HOUSTON, TEXAS

2365 Rice Boulevard, Suite 202,
Houston, Texas 77005

10 9 8 7 6 5 4 3 2 1

Library of Congress Cataloging-in-Publication Data

Chemerka, William R.

Juan Seguin : Tejano leader / by William R. Chemerka.

pages cm

ISBN 978-1-933979-79-3

1. Segumn, Juan Nepomuceno, 1806-1890—Juvenile literature.

2. Soldiers—Texas—Biography—Juvenile literature.

3. Politicians—Texas—Biography—Juvenile literature.

4. Alamo (San Antonio, Tex.)—Siege, 1836—Juvenile literature.

5. Texas—History--Revolution, 1835-1836—Biography—Juvenile literature.

6. Texas—History—Republic, 1836-1846—Juvenile literature. I. Title.

F390.S4653 2012

976.4'03092--dc23

[B]   2011052720

Illustrations by Don Collins

Printed in China through Asia Pacific Offset

Dedicated to the descendants
of Juan Seguín

TABLE OF CONTENTS

CHAPTER 1

....

Ride Like the Wind

Don Erasmo Seguín, the postmaster of San Antonio de Béxar, Texas looked at his young son, Juan, and smiled.

"May I go to school now, Father?" asked Juan.

"Yes, my son."

Don Erasmo was pleased that his son wanted to attend school, but there was no official school in the town. The last school was closed in 1793, nearly seventeen years earlier, when the Mission San Antonio de Valero church school ended its operation.

Don Erasmo knew the importance of education, so he organized a school in an abandoned one-room adobe building. It was hardly what some would call a school since it did not have a full-time teacher. Various adults from the town volunteered to teach the students how to read and write. Still, it was a place of learning.

"Remember, Juan, pay attention to the teacher," instructed Don Erasmo. "Education is important. Make your mother and me proud of you."

"If I study hard in school, will I be the *alcalde* one day?" asked Juan about the office of mayor.

"We will talk about that when you grow up,"

laughed Don Erasmo. "Now, off you go."

Juan was greeted by two of his friends, Manuel Flores and Gregorio Esparza. In an instant, the three boys raced along the dirt road towards the school.

The school room had only six wooden benches for the students. The teacher stood behind a table upon which the writing lessons were taught. Juan would carefully write his full name, Juan Nepomuceno Seguín, each day on a piece of paper.

Gregorio Esparza looked at Juan's paper.

"You made a mistake," said Gregorio as he shook his head back and forth.

"With my own name?" questioned Juan.

"Yes," said Gregorio, struggling to hide a smile. "You left out *alcalde*."

Both boys laughed.

After school, Juan helped his father in the family fields. His father always complimented him. "Good work, Juan," said Don Erasmo. "Thank you, Father," replied Juan.

When he completed his chores, Juan and his friends went horseback riding. Juan was the best rider. One day he galloped so fast that a cloud of dust kicked up and settled on the newly-washed laundry that hung from a rope at the back of his house.

"Juan!" shouted his father as the dust cloud covered him.

"Do not be angry, my husband," said María Seguín, brushing the fine particles of dirt off her husband's jacket.

"But look what he did," said Don Erasmo sternly.

"It is only dust," she reasoned. "It will come out in the next wash."

"But María," he countered.

María Seguín calmly looked at her husband. "The years will go by so quickly that one day we will remember this day with affection," she replied.

"Affection, you say?" questioned Don Erasmo. "After all your hard work, the clothes are covered with dirt. Just look at them now. And look at me."

"And look at our son," said María. "He rides like the wind itself."

Don Erasmo's angry look melted into a smile of pride as he watched Juan's horse easily jump a rail fence.

And, the years did go by.

In 1820, Don Erasmo Seguín was elected *alcalde* of San Antonio de Béxar. Juan was proud of his father. The elder Seguín was the town's most prominent office holder, and the citizens looked to him for guidance and leadership.

"It is noble to serve your community," lectured Don Erasmo to his son. "Perhaps one day you will be the *alcalde*. But you must serve with honor and always do what is right."

"Yes, Father," said Juan.

In 1821, Mexico gained its independence from Spain. The Mexican citizens established a democracy, a form of government based upon the rule of the people.

Mexico became a land of opportunity. It offered large tracts of land in Texas, one of its states, to American immigrants. The newcomers had to work the land for seven years before they could sell it. In return for the generous land offerings, the Mexican government asked the new citizens for their allegiance to Mexico and to the Catholic Church.

Thousands of Americans moved to Texas. One new arrival, Stephen F. Austin, became friends with the Seguín family. Austin brought hundreds of additional families to Texas. Don Erasmo helped Austin and other immigrants adapt to their new homeland.

Don Erasmo was elected to the Mexican Congress in 1823. The following year, the Constitution of 1824 was created. Modeled after the Constitution of the United States, the document guaranteed rights to the citizens of Mexico and limited the powers of the central government.

The new government reorganized its states. Texas was combined with neighboring Coahuila into the new state of Coahuila y Tejas. Some Texans were concerned that their representative rights were being limited because Texas was no longer its own state.

By 1824, Juan Seguín had become a young man. The 18-year-old worked on his father's property and assisted in the post office. In his free time, Juan still enjoyed horseback riding. Sometimes he would ride for hours with his friends.

During one of his rides, Juan met María Gertrudis Eusevia Flores whose father owned one of the largest ranches in San Antonio de Béxar. Gertrudis was a personable and charming young woman. Juan fell in love with her, and they married in 1826.

CHAPTER 2

···

Public Service

In 1828, Juan decided to follow in his father's footsteps and enter public service. He wanted to represent his community. Juan was well known as a responsible, hardworking young man. The citizens of San Antonio de Béxar elected him as an alderman, a municipal official.

Manuel Flores and Gregorio Esparza congratulated him.

"Well done, Juan," said Manuel.

"That's Don Juan Seguín," corrected Gregorio with a smile. "Not *just* Juan."

All three laughed.

"One day you may be *alcalde* after all," said Manuel.

"At least he can count on two votes," chuckled Gregorio.

Juan remembered what his father said about public office. He set out to honorably represent the wishes of the citizens. Juan also wanted to set an example for his growing family. Maria Cecilia Seguín was baptized on January 6, 1827; Juan was baptized on December 29, 1829. The Seguín Family eventually numbered ten children.

Texas was also growing. By 1830, the Anglo

immigrant population from the United States outnumbered the Tejano population in Texas. The new settlers
believed strongly in representative government, individual
liberty, property rights and other American traditions. But
some of Juan's neighbors were concerned that the new
arrivals from the United States would not want to adapt
to their new land.

"I feel that some of the Anglos do not see us Tejanos
as equals," remarked Manuel.

"Manuel speaks the truth, Juan," added Gregorio.
"Some do not follow our customs."

"That is not what is in the heart of my friend Jim
Bowie," replied Juan.

"Bowie is different from the other Anglos," said
Manuel. "He married into a Tejano family."

"What do you think, Juan?" asked Gregorio.

"We are all Texans now," stated Juan. "We live in a
democracy where we are free to do what we want as long
as our actions are within the law. We welcome our new
citizens."

But the Mexican government did not. In 1830,
Mexico banned immigration from the United States.

Years later, in the spring of 1833, the Texans called
for a convention in the settlement of San Felipe de Austin
to discuss the immigration ban and other concerns. At

the meeting, a few representatives suggested that Texas should be an independent state, separate from Coahuila.

Stephen F. Austin traveled to Mexico City to present the concerns of the Texans to Antonio López de Santa Anna, the newly-elected President of Mexico. But the Mexican leader had departed for one of his estates. Instead, Austin met with interim President Valentin Gómez Farias. The idea of separate statehood for Texas was rejected.

In October 1833, Austin wrote to the *ayuntamiento* (city council) of San Antonio suggesting that Texas write its own constitution separate from the other Mexican states. A month later, in a meeting with Santa Anna, Austin restated the wishes of the Texans. Once again, the separate statehood idea was rejected. However, Santa Anna repealed the ban on immigration.

Later in the year, the local election for *alcalde* was held in San Antonio de Béxar. Juan was elected.

Once again, his friends came to congratulate him.

"Your childhood dream finally came true," said Gregorio. "*Alcalde* Seguín!"

"Indeed!" replied Manuel with a broad smile.

But more problems were developing. On his return home from Mexico in January 1834, Austin was captured and imprisoned by Mexican authorities for promoting sedition against the government. Santa Anna began to ignore the Constitution. He dismissed many government officials and established a dictatorship.

In the spring of 1835, the Mexican leader brutally suppressed a revolt in the state of Zacatecas when its citizens refused to disband their militia. Many Texans were upset.

"Problems face us, my loyal friends," said Juan at a meeting in his house. "Santa Anna has vowed to stop all dissent against his rule. And he has imprisoned all those who speak out against him."

"What shall we do?" asked Manuel.

"Shall we join with the Anglos who protest against Santa Anna?" questioned Gregorio.

"We will stand up and take back the rights under the Constitution of 1824 that Santa Anna has taken away from us," stated Juan. "We will join forces with all who wish to stand against tyranny."

"Be careful, Juan," warned Gregorio. "You have more to lose than we do. You have a large ranch and many horses. And your father's land could also be forfeited to Santa Anna."

"My father always told me to do what is right," noted Juan. "Texas must be its own state, and we must have our freedoms. Are you with me?"

"Of course," said Manuel.

"And you can count on me, too," replied Gregorio. "I

know of others who will join us."

Austin was finally released from prison. He returned to Texas a changed man. He was no longer willing to peacefully negotiate with Santa Anna's government. "We must defend our rights, ourselves, and our country by force of arms," declared Austin. Don Erasmo, Juan's father, agreed and pledged to supply any volunteer military force that Austin organized and commanded.

At home, Juan's wife expressed concern over the growing political tensions.

"Juan, you and your father face grave danger if Santa Anna were to send his large army here," said Gertrudis. "If something terrible happened, what would our children do without a father and a grandfather?"

Juan carefully thought about what Gertrudis had said. He took his wife by the hand and looked into her eyes. "Our children will be fine," replied Juan. "I will protect them and you. Always."

CHAPTER 3

....

The Texas Revolution Begins

Santa Anna believed that the Anglos in Texas were starting a revolution, much like the revolt in 1776 that gave birth to the United States. Santa Anna ordered the imprisonment of all who opposed his rule.

In October 1835, Santa Anna's military commander in Texas, General Martín Perfecto de Cos, sent a cavalry detachment to Gonzales to confiscate a cannon. But when the mounted Mexican troops arrived, the Texans confronted them with a flag that stated "Come And Take It!" Gunshots were exchanged and the Mexican cavalry retreated. The Texas Revolution had begun.

Following the outbreak of hostilities at Gonzales, Austin commissioned James Bowie as a colonel of infantry and Juan as a captain of cavalry in the newly-created Texas army. Juan quickly recruited over three dozen men, including many of his friends and neighbors like Manuel Flores, Gregorio Esparza, Plácido Benavides and Antonio Cruz y Arocha.

General Cos threatened to punish all those who supported the revolution against Mexico. However, Austin had plans of his own. He planned to fight General Cos. Austin ordered Bowie into action.

On October 28, 1835, Juan's company joined Bowie's men near Mission Concepción which was located a few miles outside of San Antonio.

"We are so close that they must know we are here," said Juan to Bowie.

"And Cos must know that we have fewer than 100 men," replied Bowie. "We'll be ready."

General Cos sent fewer than 100 men against them.

"Keep under cover, boys, and reserve your fire," shouted Bowie. "We haven't a man to spare." Cannons, rifles and muskets fired for a half an hour. Although outnumbered, the Texans and Tejanos won the Battle of Concepción. At his headquarters, General Cos wondered what would happen next.

Following the battle, Austin ordered Juan's company to scout the countryside and assist in supplying the troops. Don Erasmo also helped by providing supplies to Austin's growing volunteer army. However, Austin soon left Texas to seek assistance from the United States. General Edward Burleson took command.

In early December 1835, Burleson organized an attack against General Cos's troops who were stationed in San Antonio de Béxar and in the Alamo. Burleson gave Juan the responsibility to prevent any Mexican soldier from entering or leaving the area.

The Battle of Béxar began on December 5, 1835. The fighting in the streets continued throughout the day and early evening. The air was filled with musket balls and artillery projectiles. Local families fled from house to house as the rival forces engaged in combat. The gunfire trailed off at dusk. Juan warned his men that General Cos would probably send out messengers during the night.

When it was dark, Juan positioned his men in small groups around the Alamo where General Cos was head-quartered. The old mission's courtyards were illuminated by dozens of campfires.

"It looks peaceful," said Juan.

"For tonight, perhaps," remarked Plácido.

Suddenly, a Mexican rider emerged from the Alamo's main gate and headed south.

"We must stop him!" exclaimed Juan.

"He won't get through our lines," replied Plácido.

"Let's ride!" shouted Juan.

Juan led one group of mounted volunteers towards the rider; Plácido led another. Mexican soldiers started to fire from the walls of the Alamo. The rider noticed the two groups of Tejanos closing in on him. He quickly turned his horse and galloped back inside the gate. Musket shots continued to ring out. Juan ordered his men away from musket range.

"That was a close call," said Manuel.

"But no one was hurt and the rider remains inside the Alamo," said Juan. "Good work. But Cos will try again. Be on your guard until sunrise, amigos."

The Battle of Béxar continued for several days. Cannon blasts and musket volleys thundered. The house-to-house fighting in town was particularly difficult. Texans and Tejanos fought side by side amid crumbling walls and abandoned houses as they battled the veteran Mexican soldiers. When artillery help was needed, Gregorio Esparza volunteered to serve on one of the Texan cannon crews.

As Mexican casualties increased, General Cos ordered his men in town to retreat back inside the Alamo. General Burleson's men surrounded the old mission. Mexican supplies and ammunition were running low. Once again, Juan and his mounted volunteers prevented Mexican messengers from leaving the Alamo.

Finally, on December 10, 1835, General Cos surrendered. He promised to honor the Constitution of 1824 and not return to Texas. The victorious Texans and Tejanos celebrated as they took control of the Alamo and its cannons.

General Burleson congratulated Juan. "You have performed well, Captain Seguín," said the commander. "Thank you, General," replied Juan. "But it was the men who served with me who have earned the glory."

CHAPTER 4

....

A Peaceful Winter

After General Cos and his soldiers left San Antonio de Béxar, most Texan and Tejano volunteers returned to their homes. A small group of Texans remained in the Alamo under the command of Lieutenant Colonel James Neill.

It was a peaceful winter. Soon Christmas arrived. Christmas was a wonderful holiday in San Antonio de Béxar. After attending church services, Juan and his family returned home and enjoyed a delicious dinner prepared by Gertrudis.

"The best part of this Christmas is that you are safe, Juan," said Gertrudis with a smile. "We are all safe."

"Indeed we are," replied Juan.

"It is good that General Cos is gone," said Gertrudis. "But will he return?"

"I do not know, my dear," answered Juan.

"I hope, for the children's sake, that he will not," replied Gertrudis. "The fighting was too close to our home. They have seen too much bloodshed and destruction."

"Remember," said Juan, "I have told you that I will always protect you and the children."

In January, Colonel James Bowie returned to San

Antonio de Béxar with orders from General Sam Houston, the commander of the Texas army, to abandon the Alamo. But Bowie was impressed with the old mission's sturdy walls and the large number of captured Mexican weapons. Instead, he urged Lieutenant Colonel Neill to defend the Alamo. Neill agreed with Bowie.

However, in February, Neill departed for home in order to care for ill family members. Before he left the Alamo, Neill wrote to Houston and told him about the support of the local Tejanos: "I can say to you with confidence that we can rely on great aid from the citizens of this town in case of attack."

Lieutenant Colonel William Barret Travis replaced Neill as Alamo commander and quickly requested reinforcements. But some of the volunteers questioned the need to stay since General Cos had promised not to return.

At the Seguín ranch one evening, Juan hosted a dinner for several of the men who served in his cavalry company. He had not seen some of them for many weeks. Juan was glad to meet with them again.

"Well, my friends, the planting season will soon be upon us," said Juan as he sat back in his large wooden chair. "Spring is always a time for renewal."

"Ah, spring!" smiled Manuel. "And Cos has been gone for over a month. He kept his word. He never came back to reclaim the Alamo."

"I fought to restore our rights under the Constitution of 1824," said Plácido. "But some of the Anglos want more. They want Texas to be independent of Mexico."

"I have heard such talk, too," said Gregorio. "Imagine that: Texas as its own country."

"It is a bold move," stated Antonio with a shrug of his shoulders. "What should we do, Juan?"

"Be prepared," said Juan.

"Prepared for what?" questioned Manuel. "Cos and his men have left Texas. There is no need to maintain a large force here in Béxar. Perhaps only a few volunteers are needed."

"Those of us here can do the job by ourselves," said Gregorio with confidence.

"You sound like General Burleson," smiled Manuel.

Juan Seguín sat forward in his chair. "Santa Anna will not appreciate what happened here last December. His army, no doubt, will be back."

Manuel's smile disappeared. "Do you think so, Juan?" he replied. For a moment, they all remained silent.

"But when?" asked Gregorio.

The answer came soon enough.

CHAPTER 5

....

Santa Anna Arrives

Santa Anna's Army of Operations was on the march. Thousands of soldiers were headed to San Antonio de Béxar to retake the Alamo and punish all who took up arms against Santa Anna's rule.

Volunteers arrived in San Antonio de Béxar to join the fight against Santa Anna. The most famous volunteer was David Crockett, the celebrated frontier congressman from Tennessee. A party was held in his honor upon his arrival. Crockett entertained everyone with tall tales about the Creek Indian War, bear hunting, and living on the frontier.

The joyous celebration was soon forgotten when the first of Santa Anna's soldiers were spotted approaching the town by Juan's scouts on February 23, 1836. Everyone was surprised that the *soldados* (soldiers) had successfully made a winter march through the snow-covered valleys and plains of northern Mexico.

Fear gripped the citizens of San Antonio de Béxar. Many people fled the community. The 150 volunteers quickly made their way inside the Alamo compound. A few, like Gregorio Esparza, brought family members with them.

Santa Anna ordered his soldiers to place a red flag on

top of the San Fernando church.

"What does that flag mean?" asked Antonio from his position above the Alamo's main gate. "It is obviously not the national flag of Mexico."

"It means no quarter," explained Juan.

"No quarter?" asked Antonio.

"No prisoners," replied Juan. "We must fight and win to live. Antonio, assemble the men."

Juan addressed the Tejanos under his command near the horse corral. He looked into the eyes of every man. "Texas shall be free, independent," he said. "Or we shall perish with glory in battle."

Travis later met with Juan and discussed the defense of the Alamo.

"We are surrounded by a thousand or more of Santa Anna's soldiers, and more will be arriving everyday," explained Travis. "We are outnumbered. We need the volunteers from Gonzales, Goliad and the other settlements. We need Houston's army, too. I have a few scouts I can count on. I may need you to ride through enemy lines and bring us reinforcements."

"I will do my best, Colonel," said Juan. "And you can rely on my men."

After his meeting with Travis, Juan spoke to the Tejanos in his company.

"The fate of the Alamo rests with us," said Juan. "We may be called to bring help here. If ordered by Colonel Travis, we will go out at night. Most of Santa Anna's soldiers will be asleep, although there will be a few mounted patrols and some *soldados* on guard duty. Above all, we must get through Santa Anna's lines."

"How will we manage that?" asked Antonio.

"Ride like the wind," answered Juan.

CHAPTER 6

....

The Siege and Battle of the Alamo

The next day, more Mexican soldiers arrived. At night, sentries on the Alamo walls anxiously looked for reinforcements. But no additional Texans came to the defense of the Alamo.

In the meantime, Mexican cannons roared. Artillery projectiles struck the stone walls of the Alamo compound; others exploded overhead. The women and children of the Alamo were placed in the mission's church building. The main area of the old church was roofless but a few side rooms were secure with thick stone walls and roofs.

Travis wrote a letter addressed to the people of Texas. "I shall never surrender or retreat," wrote Travis. "Come to our aid, with all dispatch. Victory or death."

The Alamo commander called Juan into his headquarters on February 25, the third day of the siege.

"Captain Seguín, I need you to ride and find Houston," said Travis. "You are our best hope. Take one other man with you. Leave tonight. Good luck."

"Thank you, Colonel," replied Juan. "We will do our best."

Juan went to every Tejano in the Alamo and wished

them well. He met last with Gregorio Esparza.

"Gregorio, when this is all over I expect to see you and your family at my home," said Juan with a reassuring smile.

"We look forward to it," replied Gregorio as his children gathered around him.

"Until then, adiós," said Juan.

Later that evening, Juan and Antonio Cruz y Arocha left the Alamo. The Mexican artillery was silent. Hundreds of campfires burned brightly. Juan and Antonio were not detected when they departed. However, several minutes later a Mexican cavalry patrol approached them as they rode near the town. Juan did not act nervous when the mounted soldiers surrounded him.

"*Buenas noches, senóres,*" greeted Juan. "We are fellow countrymen."

The Mexican soldiers hesitated.

"We are heading home," added Juan in a relaxed manner. "May we be on our way?"

A Mexican officer carefully looked at them. Then he nodded approval and allowed Juan and Antonio to continue. When the Mexican soldiers were out of sight, Antonio let out a deep breath. "That was close," said Antonio.

"Too close," replied Juan.

Juan and Antonio rode away. They later learned that Colonel James Fannin, who commanded four hundred armed Texans at Goliad, was not coming to the aid of the Alamo. Juan was very disappointed.

"Fannin will not reinforce the Alamo," said Antonio. "All is lost."

"Do not give up hope just yet," reasoned Juan. "We must locate General Houston and his army before it is too late."

While Juan and Antonio rode towards Houston's camp, the siege of the Alamo continued. Santa Anna's artillery crews kept up their bombardment of the old mission's walls for nearly a week. Travis wondered if Juan and Antonio successfully made it through the Mexican lines.

Help finally came to the Alamo. On March 1, 1836, thirty-two reinforcements from Gonzales arrived. Despite the addition of the new volunteers, Travis's command was still outnumbered twenty to one. Nevertheless, the Alamo defenders held on.

Texas independence was declared on March 2, 1836 at the Washington-on-the-Brazos settlement. Like the famous United States Declaration of Independence in 1776, Texas stated to the world that it was a new nation. The Alamo defenders, though, were unaware of the historic declaration which created the Republic of Texas. And, they would never find out.

Juan and Antonio finally arrived at Houston's camp in Gonzales. General Houston told Juan that his army was not yet ready to assist the Alamo defenders. Juan was very distressed. He knew that the Alamo could not hold out much longer without help.

"General, I request that I lead a company back to the Alamo with supplies," said Juan.

"You may depart tomorrow Captain Seguín," replied Houston.

Juan realized that his small group of mounted volunteers would not be large enough to properly reinforce Colonel Travis's troops. Still, he was determined to help the Alamo defenders.

The next day, March 6, Juan and his men left Gonzales for the Alamo. But on that very morning, Santa Anna's *soldados* attacked the Alamo. Once the Mexican soldiers climbed over the Alamo's exterior walls, the Texan defense collapsed. Hand-to-hand fighting continued inside the buildings and the church. But there were too many *soldados*. The desperate battle lasted for about an hour. When the fighting was over, all of the Alamo defenders had been killed. Santa Anna demanded that their bodies be burned.

When Juan and his company finally arrived at the outskirts of San Antonio de Béxar they were told by an old man what had happened at the Alamo.

"Travis, Bowie, Crockett, all gone," said the old man as Juan dismounted. "Your men, too, have been lost. Santa

Anna ordered his men to burn the bodies, except for Esparza. He was buried."

Juan was stunned by the news. Tears filled his eyes. For several minutes he remained motionless as he thought about the tragedy. He remembered the Tejanos in his company who died during the battle. He thought about Colonel Travis, Jim Bowie, Davy Crockett and the other brave Texans who perished in the fight.

Juan composed himself, mounted his horse and led his men quickly back to General Houston.

CHAPTER 7

....

The Battle of San Jacinto

There was much sadness in Sam Houston's camp when Juan's men brought the news about the fall of the Alamo. The loss of the Alamo was still painful for Juan because of his friends and neighbors who had died there. A few weeks later, the Texans learned that Colonel Fannin and his men were killed at Goliad by another large force of Santa Anna's soldiers.

Juan expected Houston to quickly form his army and march westward towards San Antonio de Béxar. Instead, Houston led his army eastward, away from the advancing Mexican soldiers. Juan questioned why Houston did not want to fight.

"Be patient, Captain Seguín," said Houston. "Our time will come."

"When that time comes, my men and I will be ready," replied Juan.

For weeks, Santa Anna's soldiers trailed Houston as the Texan commander led his troops eastward. The Mexican commander established a camp near the junction of Buffalo Bayou and the San Jacinto River on April 20.

General Santa Anna had divided his army and sent

them in different directions after the fall of the Alamo. Each part of his army searched for rebellious Texans. The Mexican leader commanded fewer than 1,000 *soldados,* but General Cos soon arrived at Santa Anna's camp with additional men. Santa Anna's force numbered nearly 1,400 soldiers; Houston had fewer than 1,000 men. Nevertheless, Houston decided it was time for action.

At first, Houston ordered Juan and his men excused from the attack. "Captain Seguín, in the chaos of battle you and your men might be mistaken for Santa Anna's men," reasoned Houston. "I would not want that to happen."

"General, some of my men died at the Alamo," declared Juan. "Santa Anna has plundered my home and those of my neighbors. He has trampled our constitution. We must be a part of the fight."

"Then be prepared, Captain," said Houston. "Tomorrow we will avenge the deaths at the Alamo and Goliad. But you must identify yourself on the battlefield. I do not want any of our newest volunteers to think you are in the Mexican ranks."

Juan found some cardboard that lined a wooden supply box. He shredded the cardboard into playing card-sized pieces. Juan distributed them to his men and asked them to attach the pieces into their hat bands or scarves.

"Wear these so fellow Texans won't mistake you for a

soldado," instructed Juan to his men.

On the afternoon of April 21, 1836, two cannons fired at the Mexican camp. The Battle of San Jacinto was underway. Texan infantry rushed across the grassy field. Mounted troops galloped ahead.

Shouts rang out within the Texan ranks: "Remember the Alamo!" "Remember Goliad!" *"Recuerden el Alamo!"* *"Recuerden La Bahía!"*

Santa Anna's soldiers fired back, but they could not stop the Texans. Houston's men quickly overran the Mexican defenses. Mexican casualties mounted. The battle turned into a rout. The *soldados* started to run away. Some jumped into a nearby lake to escape but the Texans followed. In less than twenty minutes it was over. Houston had won the Battle of San Jacinto.

Houston suffered a musket ball wound to his left ankle. As he sat against a tree, Houston was informed of the casualties. Nine Texans had been killed and approximately 30 were wounded; 630 Mexican soldiers had been killed and 208 were wounded. Houston's men also captured over 500 *soldados.*

But Santa Anna had escaped.

Houston would not claim total victory until Santa Anna was found. Patrols were organized and sent out to look for him. Santa Anna was later found hiding and brought before Houston. The Mexican general was surrounded by the Texans who wanted to punish him. Santa Anna agreed to recognize the independence of Texas. In return, Houston allowed him to return to Mexico.

Juan and several other men were entrusted by Houston to trail Santa Anna's army as it left Texas. The defeated *soldados* marched towards the Rio Grande as Juan and the others watched.

"The war is over," whispered Juan to himself. "We really have won. Texas is free."

Juan was rewarded for his military service. He later received 1,280 acres of land for his twenty-nine months of duty. Like other veterans of San Jacinto, Juan also received an additional 640 acres.

Juan returned home to his wife and children.

CHAPTER 8

....

Remembering the Alamo

The new government, the Republic of Texas, was formed in 1836. Elections were held and David Burnet became the president of the republic. Burnet promoted Juan to Lieutenant Colonel and gave him the authority to command the military government of San Antonio de Béxar until local elections established new leaders.

Juan wanted Texas to remember the sacrifices made by the men who died at the Alamo. In February, 1837, he gathered up the remaining ashes of the Alamo defenders and placed them in a single coffin. Juan participated in a funeral procession in which the ashes were carried to the San Fernando church for a proper burial.

"These remains which we have the honor of carrying on our shoulders are those of the valiant heroes who died in the Alamo," said Juan at the church ceremony. "There are your brothers, Travis, Bowie, Crockett and others whose valor places them in the rank of my heroes."

It was a sad day in San Antonio de Béxar, but Juan was thankful that Texas was free of Santa Anna's rule. He appreciated the bravery of those who died at the Alamo.

Texas also appreciated the efforts of Juan Seguín.

In 1838, the community of Walnut Springs was renamed Seguín. Juan was thankful for the honor. That same year, artist Thomas Jefferson Wright painted a portrait of Juan in his Republic of Texas uniform.

"We must always remember the defenders of the Alamo," said Juan to Manuel. "But now is the time for all of us to look ahead at the future of Texas."

Anglo and Tejano families struggled to rebuild the homes which had been damaged during the fight for independence. A number of homes had been completely destroyed.

Although some citizens feared that Santa Anna would invade Texas again, most believed that a time of peace and prosperity was at hand. The *soldados* were gone; children played in the streets once again.

Sam Houston succeeded David Burnet as President of the Republic of Texas. The First Congress of the new nation was also organized. Later, Juan was elected a senator and served in the Second Congress. His growing family and friends were proud of him. Juan represented the people to the best of his ability. He was a popular official and was re-elected to the Third and Fourth Congresses.

Texas became a place of opportunity. More people arrived every day. Farms and ranches were established. At first, Juan and his neighbors were pleased.

However, some of the new arrivals from the United States did not respect the local Tejanos. Juan was concerned that Tejano veterans of the Texas War for Independence were not treated well. Distrust grew between many of the Tejanos and the new citizens. Arguments developed and tensions increased. Lawlessness broke out. A number of Tejano ranches and farms were damaged; cattle and horses were stolen.

"I feel like a foreigner in my own land," Juan told Manuel. "It is no wonder that some of the families are leaving this area. It is not safe. I fear for the children."

"Sometimes I think we were better off under the flag of Mexico," said Manuel.

"No, Manuel," replied Juan. "We will make things better for all of us, Anglo and Tejano, under the flag of Texas."

"You should run for *alcalde* again," stated Manuel. "You have the power to bring law and order to this community."

"Perhaps," said Juan. "We shall see."

CHAPTER 9

A Difficult Decision in Mexico

Juan Seguín was elected *alcalde* of San Antonio de Béxar in 1841.

But all was not well in Texas.

The problems between some of the new Anglo arrivals and the local Tejanos continued. Established citizens continued to have their cattle, horses and crops stolen by marauding mobs of law-breakers. More Tejano families decided to move away from the threatening situation. Families sold their property for less than it was worth and left San Antonio de Béxar.

Juan also faced economic hardships. His debts mounted. He sought to pay off his debts by raising a herd of sheep. Juan wanted to purchase a herd in Mexico but he had to get permission to safely cross the border. He wrote to Mexican General Ráfael Vásquez for his approval to travel. Vásquez's reply included a threat to invade Texas.

Juan informed other community leaders of Vásquez's threat. Some were thankful that Juan alerted them to the potential danger, but others believed that he was somehow involved with the Mexican plan. Rumors spread. Some of the new arrivals in San Antonio de Béxar said that Juan was no longer loyal to Texas.

Political conflicts in Mexico also caused problems in Texas. Rival forces south of the Rio Grande River battled each other. Sometimes each side sought an advantage by gaining the assistance of Tejanos in Texas.

"We must join with anyone who will help the citizens of San Antonio de Béxar," said Juan to his old friend, Manuel.

"Some citizens question your loyalty, Juan," said Manuel. "Do you want to help them after what they have said about you?"

"I represent all the people," replied Juan. "And I seek help from all."

"No matter where they come from?" asked Manuel. "Even if they are from Mexico?"

"Yes, even Mexico," said Juan. "The Republic of Texas is so disorganized that it cannot defend our borders. Our new country cannot bring peace to the streets of our community."

General Vásquez's threat proved true. He led a military force into an undefended San Antonio de Béxar on March 5, 1842. He hoisted the Mexican flag over the town on the sixth anniversary of the Battle of the Alamo. He departed two days later after plundering the town.

Some Anglo citizens blamed Juan for Vásquez's brief occupation of their community. "I am sorry to say, Juan, that this is no longer our community," said Manuel. "That is why more Tejano families are leaving everyday. Some are even going to Mexico."

"As *alcalde,* I will try to reason with everyone," said Juan.

"It is too late for that," replied Manuel. "San Antonio de Béxar has been taken over by those who do not know of your contributions to our land. They see you as the cause of all their problems and no longer support you. Some threaten your friends, too."

The situation in San Antonio de Béxar worsened. Despite Juan's brave service in the Texas War for Independence, some called him a traitor. Others threatened him. He fled for his safety. But his friends secretly protected him. They provided a place for him to stay while angry mobs searched for him. Juan moved from neighboring ranch to ranch for several weeks. He realized that he could not live on the run forever. Juan was eventually forced to leave his home and family. He resigned as *alcalde.*

Juan assembled his family and friends. "In order to provide for your safety, I must leave all of you," said Juan. He turned to his children. "Santiago, José, all of you— help your mother and your brother and sisters while I am gone."

"Where will you go?" asked Gertrudis.

"I will seek refuge amongst my enemies," explained Juan. "I will go to Mexico."

True to his word, Juan sought refuge in Mexico. He rode south. But upon his arrival in Laredo, a town on the north bank of the Rio Grande River, Juan was arrested by Mexican authorities and placed in prison.

"Juan Seguín, you commanded enemy troops against Mexico and that is why you have been imprisoned," said General Adrian Woll, the area military commander. "And you will remain in our prison."

Juan looked up at the small window that was blocked with iron bars. The floor of the jail room was nothing more than dirt and rocks. He thought of his wife and children. Juan feared that if he remained imprisoned for a long time his wife and children would have to beg others for help. He was saddened by all that had happened.

General Woll stared at Juan through the bars for several minutes. Then he smiled at his prisoner.

"I know why you and other Tejanos have left Texas," said General Woll. "I understand what happened to your home. Perhaps there is a way to restore your community to what it was. And perhaps there is a way to set you free."

General Woll made Juan an offer. If Juan would command a group of Tejanos in a fight against Texas, he would be released from prison. Once free, he would be able to rejoin his family and return to San Antonio de Béxar.

It was a difficult decision for Juan. In fact, it was the most difficult decision of his life.

CHAPTER 10

The Return to Texas

On September 11, 1842, Juan sat on his horse not far from the outskirts of San Antonio de Béxar. He turned to look at the Tejanos in his cavalry company. Squads of Mexican soldiers stood behind them.

"Well, Seguín, we will see if you keep your word to me," said General Woll. "You and your men will lead the attack."

Juan realized the danger. He knew that during the upcoming battle he and his men would eventually be positioned between the Texans and the Mexicans. Even if he managed to survive the battle, Juan would be branded a traitor by both sides.

The battle began. Gunshots were exchanged and soldiers on both sides fell. Juan's Tejano company advanced towards a group of Texans who were positioned behind a barricade of barrels and an overturned wagon. One of the Texans recognized Juan in the Mexican ranks.

"Look, that's Juan Seguín!" shouted one Texan.

"It can't be," said another as he reloaded his rifle. "He'd never fight against Texas."

"You'd better take another look," replied the Texan. But it was true.

Juan knew that if the Mexicans won and he returned to San Antonio de Béxar, the Texans would never trust him. If the Texans won the battle and captured him, he would probably be imprisoned. Juan thought that no matter who won the battle he would lose.

The Mexicans recaptured the town. But a week later, another force of Texans approached. They prepared for battle several miles outside San Antonio de Béxar at Salado Creek.

General Woll was informed of the advancing Texans. He assembled his army which included Tejano volunteers from town. Although outnumbered, the Texans won the battle. Woll's forces returned to San Antonio de Béxar. Juan remained in the Mexican camp.

General Woll decided not to attack again. He ordered his men to break camp and return to Mexico. Before General Woll and his *soldados* departed, Juan met his father. Don Erasmo looked at his son and lowered his head. He was disappointed to see his son among the ranks of the invading force.

"I know what you may be thinking, Father," explained Juan. "But I was forced to make a painful decision. You must understand that my actions were not directed at Texas but only at those who have corrupted Texas."

"I understand, my son," replied Don Erasmo. "But others may not."

"Then I will write the truth and have it published for all Texans to read," said Juan. "One day, everyone will understand."

"But what will you do now, my son?" asked Don Erasmo.

"I will take my family to Mexico," answered Juan.

"And what of Texas?" asked Don Erasmo. "This is your home. This is where you were born and raised."

Juan looked at the town and the countryside. He remembered his childhood horseback rides with his friends. He remembered his wedding day. He remembered the Alamo.

"No matter where I go, I will always love Texas," said Juan. "Texas is my home."

CHAPTER 11

....

Redemption

While Juan lived in Mexico, Texas joined the United States. On December 29, 1845, the Republic of Texas was annexed by the United States and became the 28th state in the Union. Mexico, though, did not officially recognize Texas as either a state of the United States or an independent republic.

Even if Mexico had acknowledged Texas's new status, it did not accept its southern border. Mexico claimed the Nueces River as Texas's southern border. Texas claimed the Rio Grande, which was further south, as its southern border. The disputed land in-between was claimed by both countries.

War broke out between the United States and Mexico in the spring of 1846 when American troops were attacked by Mexican soldiers in the disputed land. As a result of the fight, James Polk, President of the United States, asked Congress to declare war against Mexico. Congress obliged and President Polk sent thousands of troops into Mexico.

The fighting raged across Mexico. Juan and his fellow Tejanos fought alongside the Mexican forces. It was a costly war. Despite the numerous battles, more soldiers died from disease and illness than enemy weapons. By the late summer of 1847, American troops had conquered Mexico City. The fighting ended. Juan was grateful that he had survived.

On February 2, 1848, the Treaty of Guadalupe Hidalgo officially ended the war. The United States won a large amount of Mexican territory. The new land included most of today's southwestern states of the United States, from Texas to the Pacific Ocean. The boundary between Mexico and the United States was established at the Rio Grande River.

Juan wanted to return to Texas. Despite his participation in various Mexican military operations he thought he would be forgiven by most Texans. He also believed that his previous service in Texas's successful fight for independence would be held in high regard by those who remembered the Alamo.

Juan contacted officials in the United States government who might be able to help him return to Texas. He even wrote to Sam Houston who had been elected a United States senator.

Confident of his support from people like Houston, Juan returned to Texas. He established a new home on land next to where his father had once lived. Juan was glad to be in Texas once again. Many Texans still supported him. They remembered his participation at the Battle of San Jacinto. He was elected a justice of the peace in 1852. However, Texas still suffered from the lawlessness that had forced him to leave years earlier.

Juan's father died in 1857. Don Erasmo Seguín was remembered as a "true-hearted man" by both Tejano and Anglo Texans. "He has lived a full life and I mourn his passing," said Juan. "But I will forever be grateful to him."

The next year, Juan published his personal memoirs. The book detailed everything that happened to him between 1834, the year before the Texas Revolution, and 1842, the year when he returned to San Antonio de Béxar with General Woll.

"I owe it to myself, my children and friends, to answer them with a short, but true exposition of my acts," wrote Juan. He believed that the book would help restore his reputation among those who doubted him.

However, a larger drama was developing. The issue of slavery was dividing the United States. Many in the northern states were opposed to slavery. In fact, in 1860, Presidential candidate Abraham Lincoln stated that slavery should not be extended into the new territories acquired by the United States.

Slavery, though, was allowed in Texas. Some Texans threatened to break away from the United States if the federal government attempted to end slavery. Abraham Lincoln won the presidential election. One month later, South

Carolina proclaimed its separation from the United States.

During the winter of 1860-61, the Texas state legislature discussed the possibility of breaking away from the United States. Sam Houston, the governor of Texas, warned against any action that would separate Texas from the national government.

Despite Houston's warning, Texas seceded from the United States in February 1861. Texas voters endorsed the secession decision with an official declaration on March 2, the 25th anniversary of Texas Independence. Texas promptly joined the Confederate States of America.

The Civil War began on April 12, 1861. The flag of the Confederate States of America was soon raised in San Antonio de Béxar. Once again, Texas was involved in a war. Juan, however, did not take up arms during the War Between the States. Most Texans who participated in the war fought on battlefields in other states.

The military and economic might of the United States could not be matched by the Confederate States. Yet, the southern states fought on. The war ended in 1865. The Confederate States of America dissolved and the rebellious states were eventually re-admitted into the Union. Slavery was banned. Juan was glad that the war had ended.

Four years later, Juan, now 62 years old, was elected as a judge in Wilson County, Texas. He was pleased to receive the confidence of the voters.

"Father, I am proud of you," said Santiago.

"Thank you, my son," replied Juan. "The citizens must have sympathy for an old man."

"You are not old, Father," smiled Santiago.

The Seguíns eventually sold their Texas property and moved to Nuevo Laredo, Mexico. The town was situated across the Rio Grande River from Laredo, Texas. Nuevo Laredo was Juan's final home.

In 1874, the Texas State Legislature declared Juan a hero of the Texas War for Independence. His family and friends thought the acknowledgement was long overdue. Others thought differently. They remembered when he served in the Mexican ranks under General Woll.

The years went by. By 1890, the nation had 44 states and a population of nearly 63,000,000. Over 2,000,000 people lived in Texas. Railroads connected the Atlantic and Pacific coasts.

Juan died in Nuevo Laredo on August 27, 1890. He was 83 years old. But the Mexican town was not his final resting place. In 1974, his remains were carefully moved to Seguin, Texas. An official ceremony celebrated Juan Seguín's final burial place on July 4, 1976, the 200th anniversary of the United States of America.

Juan Seguín was finally home. In Texas.

THE SEGUÍN LEGACY

Juan Seguín is memorialized in many ways. Seguin, Texas, of course, is named after him. Schools, highways and roads also bear the name of the famous Tejano leader. In 1944, the ship *S.S. Juan N. Seguin* was commissioned.

The Texas State Historical Survey Committee erected a marker to honor Juan Seguín outside City Hall in Seguin, Texas in 1970

The marker reads:

Juan Nepomuceno Seguin
(1806-1890)

Born in San Fernando De Béxar (San Antonio), son of Erasmo Seguín, whose ancestors came to America about 1700. Juan N. Seguín and his father in 1834 rallied fellow Texans against dictator Santa Anna. Young Juan Seguin raised Tejano troops, and fought in the Siege of Bexar, 1835. He provided horses for soldiers of Col. W. B. Travis, further aiding as a courier during the Siege of the Alamo.

Between the fall of the Alamo and the Battle of San Jacinto, he led his Co. A, 2nd Regiment, Texas cavalry, as rear guard for Gen. Sam Houston, protecting the civilians fleeing in front of the army of Santa Anna. His men and Mosley Baker's troops held San Felipe, preventing the Mexican army from crossing the Brazos there. Seguin's unit joined Gen. Sam Houston's army and fought at the Battle of San Jacinto.

In May 1836, Seguin gave military burial to the ashes of the heroes of the Alamo. From 1837 to 1840 he served the Republic of Texas as a senator.

The town of Walnut Springs, on the Guadalupe, changed its name (Feb. 25, 1839) to "Seguin," to honor this hero.

Juan Seguin married Maria Gertrudis Flores. At his death he was buried in Nuevo Laredo, where his grave is cared for by citizens of the city of Seguin.

THE JUAN SEGUÍN MONUMENT

On October 28, 2000 a larger-than-life statue of Juan Seguín was unveiled in Seguin, Texas. The bronze sculpture depicts the uniform-wearing Tejano leader mounted on a horse. The statue was designed by Erik Christianson. It measures ten-feet high and ten-feet wide. Including its base, the monument reaches a height of 17 feet.

....

JUAN SEGUÍN ON TV AND IN MOTION PICTURES

Juan Seguín has been portrayed by a number of different actors in TV productions and motion pictures over the years:

Joseph Calleia, *The Alamo* (1960)
A. Martinez, *Seguin* (PBS 1982)
Michael Wren, *The Alamo: Thirteen Days to Glory* (NBC 1987)
Derek Caballero, *Alamo…The Price of Freedom* (1988)
Jordi Mollá, *The Alamo* (2004)

AUTHOR'S NOTE

Whenever possible the actual words from Juan Seguín's *Personal Memoirs* were used as dialogue in this book. Seguín spoke Spanish. His conversations with other historical figures mentioned in this book, like General Sam Houston and Alamo commander William Travis, were conducted through translators.

Thanks to Rusty Gamez of the Daughters of the Republic of Texas Alamo Library, the staff of Bright Sky Press, and the descendants of Juan Seguín who continue to honor their most famous ancestor.

A special "thank you" to Albert Seguín C. Gonzales, 3rd great-grandson of Juan Seguín, for his assistance, support, encouragement and friendship.

I am indebted to Dr. J. F. de le Teja, Professor and Chairman, Department of History, Texas State University – San Marcos, for his suggestions and guidance. He is the State Historian of Texas and the author of *A Revolution Remembered: The Memoirs and Selected Correspondence of Juan N. Seguín.*